"Let the beauty of the Lord our God be upon us."

Psalm 90:17

Inspirational Images

BY J. LLOYD EWART

DEDICATED TO OUR CHILDREN'S CHILDREN – OUR FUTURE

THANKS

to all who have encouraged my photographic efforts, especially my wife, Nancy, who also snaps shutters at my side. Thanks also to Tim Griffith of Greer Wood Products and Art Gallery, Bradshaw Mountain Photo Co., Prescott Camera Club, the United Methodist Church and a most supportive family.

About the author:

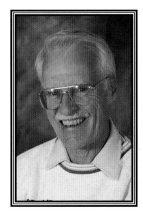

A retired United Methodist minister, Lloyd has had a life long love of the great out of doors. He has worked in forestry in Idaho, has been an avid hiker and back-packer, leading youth wilderness camps for the church, always carrying his camera along the woodland and desert trails. Since retirement Lloyd's photos have won numerous ribbons and awards, been published in calendars and enjoyed many gallery sales of prints.

© 1997 J. Lloyd Ewart
Published by: IMAGES BY LLOYD
Design: Danny Zackery & Pamela Fraser
Printing: National Promotions & Advertising
4117 West Jefferson Boulevard
Los Angeles, CA 90016
ISBN: 0-9656455-0-9

PHOTOS
Above:
Bear Berry In Tundra, Denali Park, Alaska
Cover Photo:
Tornado bearing storm clouds over Mingus Mountain,
Dewey, Arizona
Back Cover Photo:
Rainbow over Bunch Lake, Greer, Arizona
Title Page Photo:
Sunset, White Mountains, Greer Arizona

PRELUDE

In this fast paced, plastic, microchip culture, dominated by internet, T.V. and satellite dishes, we rush from place to place and often fail to find our roots in the created order. Cars speed by forests, deserts, mountains and streams missing the "statement" these wild areas are making to us about the origins and purpose of our life. We hurry past the wild flowers, the mountains, the deer. We carry the pressures and stresses of modern life along with us. Even when we travel to a mountain retreat, we often bring our city noises and modern "conveniences" with us, distancing ourselves from the "theology of wilderness." This book attempts to enable us to experience once again this precious gift of creation, of life, of love and spirit.

Some astronomers say we may be alone in this galaxy. That this planet, filled with life, is an extremely rare event. If so, all the more we must preserve its beauty which speaks to our inner self as nothing else.

I hope these images will cause you to pause a moment and reflect on life and perhaps sense something of the mood and inspiration I felt ... when I viewed these scenes through my camera viewfinder.

These images are reflections of natures' prayer for us all.

Sunset, Little Colorado River Lake, Greer, Arizona

Galapagos Hawk

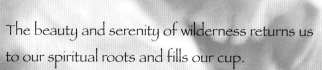

The beauty and serenity of wilderness returns us to our spiritual roots and fills our cup.

Little Colorado River, Greer Arizona

Aspen tree trunks near Alpine, Arizona

Photo by Nancy Ewart

Ever creating God of life, our prayer is one of awe and amazement at the intricate soul stirring beauty of the world around us. Thank you for reminding us with vast forests and even a single leaf that we are part of a wondrous loving universe.   AMEN

Aspen Leaf, Hall Creek, Arizona

"All things were made by Him and without
Him was not anything made that was made."
John 1:3

"The course of nature is the Art of God..."
Edward Young

The theology of nature leaps out to us in
such scenes as these.

A Glacier Falls in Canada

Lake Louise, Canada

"Consider how the lillies grow in the fields... I tell you even Solomon in all his splendour was not attired like one of these."

Matthew 6:29

The butterfly symbolizes the fact that new life, new beginning, is always offered to us.

In the desert near Tucson, Arizona

Wildflowers,
Bunch Lake,
Greer, Arizona

"How lovely is thy dwelling place O lord of hosts."   Psalm 84:1

Kootenay River, Canada

Photo by Nancy Ewart

How beautiful upon the mountains are the feet of him that bringeth good tidings, that publisheth peace: that bringeth good tidings of good, that publisheth salvation; that saith unto Zion, thy God reigneth!

Isaiah 52:7

Glacier Park, Canada

"God has made everything beautiful in its time. He has also set eternity in the hearts of people. Yet they cannot fathom what God has done from beginning to end."

Ecclesiastes 3:11

Arches National Park, Utah

Humans cannot create something like this,
but can only receive it as a gift... a treasure to preserve.

Arches National Park, Utah

Aspen trees near Big Lake, White Mountains, Arizona

Receive now, this precious gift wrapped up in glorious color, created for the express purpose of lifting our spirits and stirring our soul.

May Peace enter your heart.

Fall leaves, White Mountains, Arizona

"There is a serene and settled majesty in the Woodland scenery that enters into the soul and delights and elevates it, and fills it with noble inclinations."

Washington Irving

Near Alpine, Arizona

Consider the miracle of clouds.

Morning fog, Nenana River, Alaska

Consider the miracle of water.

Winter waterfalls, Tonto Creek, Arizona

"He leads me to quiet pools of fresh water.
He gives me new strength."

Psalm 23:2

Water has long been a symbol of refreshment and cleansing. To experience the sight and sound of flowing streams is to be baptized afresh in natures' beauty. We are renewed in spirit and made whole again.

Cathedral Rock on Oak Creek, Sedona, Arizona

on the Arizona desert

The metamorhphosis that transforms the lowly worm into a beautiful butterfly reminds us of the loving, miracle producing Creator always at work before us, around us and in us. To witness this marvel is to experience our own resurrection, new life, and beginning.

The water lily only briefly opens
its arms to draw the flying
insects and our amazement.
Like a ballerina she tiptoes on
the water and renews us.

Fish pond, Dewey, Arizona

White Mountains of Arizona

Discover the soul of the universe, the soul within natures' wonders and the soul within yourself.

Consider the miracle of Fall.

Escudilla Mountain, Alpine, Arizona

When we find the LOVE in creation as expressed in the natural world around us, we are wealthy beyond words.
One can be no richer and need not be.

The Mittens, Monument Valley, Arizona

Love Creates....Creation Loves.

Monument Valley, Arizona

South Rim, Grand Canyon Overlook

The mountains and canyons sing of the joy of creation and Creator. The psalmist proclaimed "I will look to the hills...and to the creator God who made them all."

Sunset, South Rim, Grand Canyon, Arizona

Nature is intimately personal when we interact and allow "her" (like a mother) to speak to our deep, sometimes hidden, inner self. When we are able to do this, we are lifted to the heights of spiritual ecstasy.

Consider the miracle of the flowers. Jesus said "the Kingdom of heaven is like the tiny mustard seed that grows up to become a tree so birds make their nests in its branches."

Lao Tzu, Confucius, Buddha, Moses, Mohammed and Jesus all went into the wilderness to find the deeper meaning of life.
They learned, with the psalmist, that the world and all that is in it belongs to the Lord;" the earth and all who live on it are his."

Psalm 24:1

Consider the miracle of the canyons.

Bryce Canyon at dawn

Here one can clearly see the central purpose and meaning for life... can you ?

"You created the moon to mark the months."

Psalm 104:19

Sabino Canyon, Tucson, Arizona

Even the desert places proclaim, in the stark beauty of its wilderness, a sense of awe and wonder at the forces behind such a place. The symbolism of the desert blooming, like the butterfly, offers us renewal and the desert within us blooms with new life.

San Pedro River, Arizona

"he pastures of the wilderness drip, the hills gird themselves with joy"
Psalm 65:12

Sonora Desert, Bagdad, Arizona

Peace! that's the word this scene surfaces in my soul! Peace. How the world yearns for peace--.
Well there it is, like a sunrise on a new day, a gift for the taking.   PEACE.....

Sunrise, Sabino Canyon, Tucson, Arizona

"All the earth worships thee."   Psalm 66:4

Denali Alpenglow, Mt. Mc Kinley, Denali Park, Alaska

God is personified in sacred writings, but long before the pen, ultimate reality, the ever creating God, was defined in the majestic mountains, trees and flowing waters.

Wonder Lake reflections, Mt. Foraker
Denali Park, Alaska

Doesn't such a place inspire one to grasp every precious moment of life, and embrace the gift of now.
The canyons and the flowers proclaim life is good, life is ours to enjoy, to love, to share...Now.!

Bryce Canyon at dawn, Utah

"Thou hast been our dwelling place.....before the mountains were brought forth..."

Psalm 90:1&2

Mingus Mountain, Arizona

Black River, Arizona

Every living creature proclaims
Gods' creating and loving essence.
Truly LOVE makes the world go around.

Hall Creek, Arizona

The essential joy of being is expressed in the
song of a bird or the call of a wild animal. This
is a symbol of the joyfulness of the natural
order permeating the whole fabric of creation.

Id Finch, Prescott, Arizona

Buffalo, Yellowstone Park

Raccoons, White Mountains, Arizona

"The trees and the woods will shout for joy. "
Psalm 96:12

Fall color near Big Lake , Arizona

We cannot improve on nature--but we can co-operate.......

Glacier National Park, Montana

Consider the miracle of rain.

Summer rain, Hall Creek, Greer, Arizona

"When the rainbow appears in the clouds,
I will see it and remember the everlasting
covenant between me and all living beings
on earth."   Genesis 9:16

Natures' final prayer of the day- creations' benediction.

The Alaska Range, Denali Park

To be spiritually minded is life and peace." Romans 8:6

Never lose an opportunity of seeing anything that is beautiful for beauty is God's handwriting – a wayside sacrament. Welcome it in every fair face, in every fair sky, in every fair flower, and thank God for it as a cup of blessing." Ralph Waldo Emerson

Wasatch Mountain, Utah

It took eons of time to sculpt such as these mountains. When one contemplates the fact that millions of years pass before such unique beauty unfolds before us, we tap into the creator's eternity and recognize we, too, are a part of this ongoing adventure called life.

Canyon DeChelly, Navajo Reservation, Arizona

Those who discover the miraculous riches in the created order have experienced LOVE surfacing in the midst of natures wonderul wilderness.

"I will remember your great deeds, Lord: I will recall the wonders you did in the past."

Psalm 77:11

Grand Falls, Little Colorado River,
Navajo Reservation near Flagstaff, Arizona

And the glory of the Lord shall be revealed, and all flesh
shall see it together: for the mouth of the Lord hath spoken it."
Isaiah 40:5, Handel's Messiah

Rock formations in Arches National Park, Utah

"Come unto him all ye that labour and are heavy laden,
and he will give you rest."

Matthew 11:28

Sunset over River Reservoir

Greer, Arizona

There is spirit in humankind: and the inspiration of the Almighty gives them understanding."

Job 32:8

"You shall know the truth and the truth shall make you free."

John 8:32

Peach Blossom, photo by Nancy Ewart

Some say the cosmos is a random, mindless and chaotic process, that the billions of light years of swirling, colliding violent galaxies have no direction or purpose. They say reality is a serendipitous accident with no meaning. How do we then explain the emotions humans experience when we view the Milky Way, see a photo of earth from outer space, a majestic mountain range or a tiny leaf? This is the reason we raise the "why" questions and our spirits soar beyond the physical universe in the quest for ultimate reality, which we call God, for want of a better term. Certainly this is the "stuff" of religion, faith and love. Let us climb a mountain and open our eyes.

Nothing more needs to be said.